A Veg for All Seasons

simple, seasonal recipes

Andrea Leeman

Stephen Morris

First published in 2014 by Stephen Morris
www.stephen-morris.co.uk

orders: andreavegforallseasons@btinternet.com
© Andrea Leeman

ISBN 978-0-9930554-0-9

British Library Cataloguing-in-Publication Data
A catalogue record for this book is available from the British Library.

Cover design and typesetting © Stephen Morris
Photos pages 51 and 59 © Stephen Morris

INTRODUCTION

Welcome to *A Veg for All Seasons*, a book inspired in part by 'Reg the Veg' in Clifton, Bristol. The shop's fortunes have waxed and waned over the years but in 2009 the Hagon family took over; son Tom and his wife Beth and Tom's father John with his wife Julie as book-keeper. Their displays of fruits and vegetables, much of them locally grown, are a constant delight to those who know Boyces Avenue with its archway, cafés and old arcade. One day whilst browsing the barrow outside the shop – the heaps of fresh spinach, sweet chestnuts from Somerset, Jerusalem artichokes, local medlars, apples, asparagus, beans and cabbages – a customer commented that she felt it was akin to a French market; it was a compliment from the heart. The Hagon family say it's important to their customers that a lot of the produce is organic and/or pesticide-free, and its quality certainly reflects their aim.

Initially I had in mind the book should be strictly local but this purist notion proved unreasonable as imported fruit and vegetables are essential from time to time, oranges and lemons being prime examples. At home we try to stick to seasonal produce for the good reason that it tastes better, fresher and fits the mood and the weather – no overblown Christmas strawberries for me. So the book has taken its shape from a year in my kitchen, from Windy City soup for a winter day to spring-like asparagus and broad bean risotto, through the summer fruits and vegetables and autumnal pear tatin and bottled plums.

It is not a vegetarian book, merely based on vegetables, fruits and herbs. The recipes are as straightforward as possible on the premise that fresh quality produce needs little help from the cook. Basic equipment involves sharp knives, a steamer, good olive and sunflower oil, sea salt and black pepper. Measurements are mostly metric with the occasional quirky exception such as in the making of marmalade.

Andrea Leeman

E: andreavegforallseasons@btinternet.com

The recipes

Almond and orange cake

10-12 PEOPLE

Slivers of this cake are delicious served with caramelized oranges and a generous blob of crème fraîche.

200g ground almonds

200g light brown muscovado sugar

75g self raising flour

200g unsalted butter

1 big orange – finely grate the zest and squeeze the juice

4 eggs

syrup

orange juice

2 tbsp light brown muscovado sugar

Pre-heat oven to 180C/gas mark 4

Use a 22cm/10" greased spring form cake tin, or smaller if you want a deep cake.

1. Put the almond in a bowl with the brown sugar and flour. Beat the butter and orange zest and gradually add the eggs. Add the almond and flour mixture, half at a time. Spoon into the cake tin, smooth the top and bake for 45-50 minutes until golden and just firm to the touch.

2. To make the syrup, heat the orange juice and muscovado sugar and stir until the sugar has dissolved and the juice is simmering. Remove the cake from the oven, make a dozen small holes in the top and pour over the juice whilst the cake is still in the tin. Remove when cold. Dust with icing sugar before serving.

Apple fritters in cider batter served with cinnamon and sugar

MAKES ABOUT 16 FRITTERS

4 Coxes apples

150g plain flour

1 level tsp baking soda

1 tsp caster sugar

1 egg, white and yolk separated

200mls sparkling cider, medium-sweet

sunflower or corn oil for frying

to serve

caster sugar

ground cinnamon

1. Peel the apples, cut into rings about 1cm in thickness and remove the core from the centre. Each apple makes about 4-5 rings.

2. Sift the flour, baking soda and caster sugar into a bowl. Tip the egg yolk into the centre and gradually add the cider, whisking the flour into the liquid from the centre outwards. Don't over-beat the batter; it should be the consistency of paint, not too thick and not too thin! Add more cider if it seems too thick.

3. To cook, heat sufficient oil in a frying pan for the fritters to be covered as they cook. (The oil is hot enough to cook with when a teaspoon of batter dropped into it rises to the top and puffs up into a crispy ball.) Beat the egg white and fold into the batter. Dust the apple rings in flour, dip each in the batter and fry in the hot oil, turning half way through cooking. Drain on kitchen roll and keep in a low oven until they are all ready.

4. To serve, dredge each with caster sugar and sprinkle with a pinch of cinnamon. They are delicious with vanilla ice cream.

Apricot chutney

MAKES 3 X 1LB JARS

I am a wimp about sultanas, currants and raisins and whereas I have never minded abandoning Christmas puddings and mince pies, I have spent a lifetime feeling resentful about chutney. Here is a delectable chutney recipe with not so much as a hint of a dried fruit.

10 large fresh apricots

2 Coxes or Granny Smith apples

2 echalions – torpedo shallots

2 tsps mixed spice

5cm fresh ginger

1 small red chilli or 1 tsp mustard seeds

400g Demerara sugar

1 level tsp salt

4 tbsp cider vinegar

Preheat the oven to 150C/gas mark 2

1. Steep the apricots in boiling water for 5 minutes, then peel, stone and chop into largish pieces. Peel, core and chop the apples and peel and chop the shallots. Put in a casserole dish with the spice.

2. Peel the ginger and grate into the mixture; chop and add the chilli or mustard seed. Add the sugar, salt and vinegar and stir on top of the stove until the sugar has dissolved. Cover the pan with a lid and put in the oven for an hour.

3. Finish the chutney on top of the stove without the lid, bubbling gently for a further 30 minutes or until much of the liquid has evaporated.

4. Bottle in sterilized jars, cover with waxed jam papers and add a screw-top lid to each.

The chutney is at its best after a little time to mature, about 8 to 10 weeks. Delicious with cheeses and cold meats and most particularly in toasted Cheddar cheese sandwiches.

Asparagus risotto

SERVES 4

There is a moment in late spring when English asparagus coincides with the first of the broad beans and garden mint – and when vegetarians and non-vegetarians can put their elbows on the table and settle with enthusiasm for a shared dish.

1. Wash and trim the woody ends from the asparagus, cut into 1 inch lengths. Heat the olive oil and gently cook the onion until soft.

2. Add the rice and stir with the onion until it's coated with oil. Slowly add the stock, stirring continuously. When the rice has absorbed all the stock, pour in the white wine and add the asparagus pieces and beans and continue to cook and stir until the asparagus is tender. Add the fresh mint and most of the cheese. Taste the risotto and add salt and pepper accordingly.

3. Sprinkle over the last of the cheese, add a few mint leaves and a grind of black pepper; serve immediately.

450g asparagus

2 tbsp olive oil

1 medium onion, peeled and finely chopped

300g risotto rice

750ml vegetable or chicken stock

1 glass white wine

150g fresh broad beans

1 tbsp freshly chopped mint

2 tbsp grated Parmesan

salt and pepper

Asparagus tart

SERVES 4 PEOPLE

Asparagus is one of the great but short-lived luxury crops in the U.K. and the season traditionally runs from the end of April to 21st June – the longest day – after which the plants must grow their ferns and build themselves up for the next year. It's almost a seaside crop, liking salty air – and in Somerset, not far from where I live, it's blissfully happy growing in the iron-rich soil on the county's north coast. Eat it steamed, boiled, with mayonnaise, Hollandaise sauce or with fresh-grated slivers of Parmesan cheese – or make this delicious and simple tart.

375g pack all butter puff pastry

500g asparagus

50g mature Cheddar cheese, grated

extra virgin olive oil

sea salt and black pepper

Preheat the oven to 220C/gas mark 7

1. Lightly oil a baking tray approximately 25cm x 35cm. Cut the pastry in half and roll half into a rectangle to fit roughly inside the tray (the other half of the pastry will freeze). Without cutting right through the pastry, make a line round the edges of the rectangle about 2cm in from the edge and paint this border with olive oil.

2. Cut and lay the asparagus to fit across the pastry inside the line, scatter the grated cheese over the top and splash the spears with olive oil – add a little sea salt and some black pepper to taste. Bake for 25-30 minutes, until the pastry is golden.

Aubergine, thyme-baked with olive oil

SERVES 4 PEOPLE

This idea is fired by Yotam Ottolenghi's inspirational book, *Plenty*. I know of no-one more creative in the preparation of vegetables and fruits. The finished dish looks stunning with its yoghurt dressing bejewelled with pomegranate seeds – and follow-on of wonderful flavours. Removing pomegranate seeds from their shells is no longer the painstaking procedure of childhood involving a pin and a lot of patience. Halve the fruit, hold one half in the palm of your hand over a basin and tap the skin with a heavy wooden spoon, the seeds tumble out.

Preheat the oven to 200C/gas mark 6

2 aubergines

4 tbsp olive oil

fresh lemon thyme

sea salt and black pepper

100g whole plain yoghurt

1 garlic clove

1 pomegranate

1. Cut the aubergines in half including the stems and make criss-crosses in the flesh. Paint the surfaces with the olive oil until all the oil is absorbed, then grind a little sea salt and pepper over the top and add a few sprigs of fresh thyme. Place on baking parchment flesh-side-up on a baking tray and roast for 45 minutes or until the flesh is soft and the tops and edges are browning well. Remove and cool.

2. Mix the yoghurt with the garlic clove, crushed, and a little salt. Just before serving, spoon on the yoghurt, sprinkle with a few pomegranate seeds, add a zigzag of olive oil and a few thyme leaves.

Baked squash with Parmesan

A STARTER FOR 4 PEOPLE

Green gems, round green squashes, are ideal
for baking whole. They yield a good orangey
flesh and are delicious with butter and grated
cheese, or even better, with the subtle addition
of flakes of smoked fish such as haddock.

Preheat the oven to 180C/gas mark 4

1. Using a cleaver, lob the tops off the squashes as
   though decapitating a boiled egg, then replace the
   tops: bake on a tray in the top of the oven for
   about 45 minutes until the flesh is soft.

2. Scoop out all the seeds with a teaspoon and
   discard. Spoon the rest of the flesh into a bowl
   and mix with the parsley, Parmesan, cream, lemon
   juice and salt and pepper to taste. This is the point
   to add the smoked haddock if you choose. Refill
   the squashes and return to the oven for a further
   10-15 minutes. Serve immediately.

4 green gem squashes

1 tbsp chopped flat-leaf
parsley

50g freshly-grated Parmesan

2-3 tbsp double cream

juice of ½ a lemon

salt and pepper

(optional 150-200g cooked,
flaked smoked haddock)

Beetroot jelly

SERVES 6-8 PEOPLE

I make this in individual ramekins and serve with soured cream and chives as a starter. The little salad shoots in the photograph are radish – available in health food shops.

450g cooked beetroot

425ml chicken or vegetable stock

1 packet gelatine, sufficient for 600mls (1 pint)

2 tbsp red wine vinegar

2 tbsp caster sugar

finely grated zest of a small orange

salt and pepper

The sauce

150ml soured cream

1 tbsp fresh chives, finely chopped

1. Peel the beetroot and grate quite finely. Use the 425ml stock to make up the jelly according to instructions, add the vinegar. Stir in the caster sugar, orange zest, a little salt and pepper and finally the grated beetroot.

2. Set the mixture in the ramekins and refrigerate for at least 4 hours.

3. Dip the ramekins briefly into hot water and turn out onto plates. Mix the soured cream and chopped chive to make the accompanying sauce.

Candied chocolate orange peel

1. Scrub the oranges, cut them into quarters and peel, then cut the peel into long strips, 1cm or less in width.

2. Cover with cold water and simmer gently for an hour to remove the bitterness. Drain and weigh. Return to the pan together with their weight in sugar and bubble slowly for a further ¾ hour. Leave on kitchen paper to cool and dry.

3. Melt the chocolate: dip the peel in and allow the excess to drain. Arrange on baking parchment/greaseproof paper. When cold, finish hardening the fridge.

2-3 perfect, thick-skinned oranges

granulated sugar

450g good continental dark chocolate

Caramelized oranges

SERVES 4 PEOPLE

Navelina oranges are the answer to a kitchen wallah's prayer – seedless and once the peel and pith is removed, the fruit cuts cleanly into rings. They're in the shops early in the new year together with blood oranges, a colourful alternative for this recipe.

4 Navolina oranges

4 tbsp granulated sugar

4 tbsp water

1. Use a potato peeler to cut strips of peel from the fruit, followed by a sharp knife to remove the pith. Cut the oranges across in rings 1cm thick and put into a heatproof dish.

2. Save the peel from 2 oranges and cut into long, thin strips. Put into a pan, add plenty of water and simmer gently for about 30 minutes, drain and spread on kitchen roll.

3. Put the granulated sugar into a saucepan with the water, stir over a medium heat, stirring until the sugar has dissolved. When the mixture starts to bubble, toss in the strips of peel and let them simmer until the mixture begins to caramelise to a pale chestnut. Cover your hand with a tea towel and take the saucepan to a cold tap; sprinkle the hissing mixture with about 2 tbsp of cold water and pour over the oranges.

Serve with crème fraîche.

Cavalo nero

SERVES 4 PEOPLE

Cavolo nero, with its beautiful dark vitamin-packed leaves, is an Italian member of the *Brassica* family, its flavour resembling kale. Its tasty and decorative qualities make it a good accompaniment to fish, but a little goes a long way. This is a great lunch dish – add bacon lardons or chopped salami, serve with poached salmon or as part of a cold table.

1. To prepare cavolo nero in its simplest form, pull the leaves from the stalk and use a sharp knife to cut out and discard the white stems. Now roll the leaves lengthways and cut across in thin strips.

2. It can be steamed (favourite) or dropped into boiling water and cooked for 4-6 minutes until really tender. Drain, add a little butter or olive oil, sea salt and a grating of nutmeg.

3. Peel and finely chop the onion and blanch in boiling water for 30 seconds – it takes out the sting; run under cold water and drain immediately. Deseed and chop the chilli. Halve the tomatoes, mix with the beans and other ingredients. Chop and add some of the oregano or basil.

4. Mix together in a big bowl, add the olive oil, lemon juice and seasoning and mix once more. Decorate with more oregano.

100g cavalo nero

1 small red onion

½ small green chilli, chopped

12 cherry tomatoes

100g cooked and shelled edamame or broad beans

fresh oregano or basil

2 tbsp olive oil

½ lemon

sea salt and black pepper

Braised celery

SERVES 4 PEOPLE

Like cucumber, celery simply braised is an excellent vegetable.

head of celery

stock cubes

1. Top the celery and snap the bottom bits off so that you can pull away the stringy bits. Wash and cut into 2cm pieces.

2. Dissolve 2 chicken or vegetable stock cubes in 500ml water and simmer the celery until it begins to go translucent.

3. Drain and serve immediately.

Celeriac soup

SERVES 4-6 PEOPLE

This funny, rough-hewn root vegetable may look unpromising but it makes up for looks with delicious flavours, both as a soup, raw in salads and mashed with potato. A steamer for vegetables is great news because the remaining water in the pan after steaming makes a good basic stock for soups. This recipe for a winter warmer is cooked entirely in a steamer.

top of the steamer

400g celeriac, peeled weight

1 medium potato, peeled

1 large onion, peeled

bottom of the steamer

1 carrot, peeled

1 bay leaf

2 thyme sprigs

½ fresh lemon

1 chicken stock cube

1 litre water

salt, pepper and celery salt

single cream

2 tbsp chopped chives or parsley

1. Cut all the peeled vegetables into chunks. Put the celeriac, potato and onion into the top half of the steamer and the carrot, bay leaf thyme, half lemon, stock cube and water in the bottom part. Steam until the celeriac, potato and onion are cooked.

2. Spoon the thyme, lemon and bay leaf from the water and discard. Blend the contents from the top half and bottom half of the steamer together, add salt, pepper and 1 level tsp of celery salt or a good grating of nutmeg.

3. Stir in the cream and chopped chives and serve immediately.

Celery, tomato and echalion sauce

For roasting or poaching white fish

SERVES 4 PEOPLE

see photograph on previous page

Echalions are the long torpedo-shaped shallots. An excellent base
sauce in which to cook fresh white fish such as chunks of flaky cod,
sea bream fillets or whole sea bass. Pep it up with half a chopped chilli.

4 celery sticks

4 tomatoes

2 echalions

bunch flat leaf parsley

2 tbsp olive oil

200ml dry white wine such as
Muscadet

sea salt and black pepper

1. String and chop the celery sticks in half lengthways,
then into small half-moons. Make 3-4 slashes in the
tomatoes, put into a bowl and pour over boiling
water; after a couple of minutes, run under the
cold tap, skin and remove the hard core at the top
before chopping into pieces. Peel and chop the
shallots and chop the parsley.

2. Spoon the olive oil into a pan and heat; add the
celery, tomatoes and shallots, fry gently until the
vegetables soften. Pour in the wine and cook for
another 3 minutes before adding the chopped
parsley and salt and pepper to taste.

3. Pour the sauce into a suitable dish for roasting or
steaming the fish – if steaming the pan will need a
lid. Lay the fish on the sauce and spoon a little
over the top of each fillet. Oven time is about 20
minutes in a medium oven, poaching on the stove
takes approximately 5-6 minutes on a low heat,
but don't forget to cover the fish so the steam can
do its work.

Chanterelle mushrooms with scrambled eggs

SERVES 4 PEOPLE

St George's mushrooms herald the new season's fungi in April and *Cantharellus cibarius* and *Cantharellus tubaeformis*, alias Chanterelles, bring it to a close in December with what most chefs would agree is a flourish of flavours and a grand finale. Chanterelle mushrooms make a great contribution to stews and soups but favourite is eating them with scrambled eggs, just one of those combinations that is a natural.

1. Mix a little olive and sunflower oil together and fry the Chanterelles at quite a high heat until they begin to reduce in size and are golden at the edges. Slow frying makes them soggy and spoils the texture.

2. Add a little salt and pepper and pile on to toasted muffins and scrambled eggs.

100g Chanterelle mushrooms

sunflower and olive oil

sea salt and black pepper

scrambled eggs

toasted, buttered muffins

Chestnut stuffing

SERVES 6-8 PEOPLE

Fresh sweet chestnuts are nicer than any of the pre-prepared commercial varieties. The preparation needs patience but it pays off! I prefer stuffing made in a separate dish rather than cooking it in the bird; this version is as good with roast chicken or pork as it is with turkey or goose.

2 shallots

25+g butter

1 peeled, diced cooking apple

1 tbsp (mixed) parsley, sage and thyme

175g coarse white breadcrumbs

salt and pepper

1. Peel and finely chop the shallots. Melt the butter and gently fry the shallots until soft, add the apple and herbs. Cook for a minute, stir in the bread-crumbs and seasoning.

2. Butter a baking dish and spoon in the mixture. Bake below the roasting bird for an hour. Remove and cover with tinfoil. Re-heat at the last minute if necessary.

Peeling and freezing fresh chestnuts

1. Make a slit across the bottom of the chestnut. Drop 4-5 chestnuts at a time into boiling water for a couple of minutes.

2. Run under the cold tap and remove peel and bitter pith around the nut. Freeze in an airtight container.

In a microwave

You can also use a microwave although I think it changes the texture of the chestnuts. To use it, make a slit across the bottom of the fruit and cook on high for about 30-40 seconds.

Courgette frittata

SERVES 4 PEOPLE

Courgettes frittatas are crisp fried batons of courgettes, delicious with simple fish and meat dishes – and very moreish. The preparation is easier and the cooking more consistent if you have an attachment on a mandolin for cutting vegetable sticks evenly. Salting the courgettes extracts some of the moisture, giving a crisp rather than soggy end result.

1. Wash and top and tail the courgettes. Cut into neat batons, about the size of a French *frite*. Spread the batons on a plate and sprinkle with fine salt. Leave for 30 minutes, rinse thoroughly in cold water, drain in a sieve and dry on kitchen paper.

2. Spoon the flour into a plastic bag. Heat enough oil to cover the base of a large frying pan, sufficient for shallow frying.

3. Drop the courgettes into the bag of flour and give them a good shaking to cover evenly with flour; scatter onto a plate. Add little by little to the hot fat and turn occasionally until golden at the edges and crispy.

4. Drain on kitchen paper and serve immediately.

3 courgettes

3 tbsp plain flour

fine table salt

sunflower oil for frying

Cucumber, braised with chives

SERVES 4 PEOPLE

Cucumber, lightly cooked in chicken stock and chopped chives transforms into a delicate vegetable to serve with most fish dishes, particularly salmon and white fish.

1 cucumber

1 stock cube

1 tbsp chopped chives

1. Peel the cucumber and cut into 5cm lengths. Core out the centre, halve the cucumber pieces lengthways and then cut into half-moon pieces, about 1cm thick.

2. Dissolve the stock cube with 200ml water and stir well. Add the cucumber and chives, simmer gently for about 5 minutes or until the cucumber is just becoming translucent.

Cucumber, mint and yoghurt soup

SERVES 3-4 PEOPLE

Refreshing, lightly luscious summer soup – and the simplest recipe to assemble. Add a few prawns to make it more substantial.

1. Peel the cucumber, cut into 5cm chunks and core out the seeds. Cut in half again and put in a bowl, sprinkle with 3-4 tsp salt and leave for 15 minutes.

2. Wash the cucumber in cold water and drain. Tip into a food processor with the yoghurt, milk and mint and whiz.

3. Chill and serve with a few prawns and a sprig of mint.

1 cucumber

salt

450g pot live yoghurt

150ml milk

1 tbsp freshly chopped mint

mint for decoration

Danish pickled cucumber

SERVES 6 PEOPLE

Simple to make, a delicious texture in salads, flavoursome with prawns, egg mayonnaise, in soups or served as part of a cold table. Think Danish smørrbrød, and it wouldn't seem complete without this marriage of dill and crunchy cucumber.

It will keep for 2-3 days in the fridge.

1 cucumber

1 tbsp fine table salt

2 tbsp caster sugar

2 tbsp boiling water

2 tbsp white wine or cider vinegar

2 tsp finely chopped dill

black pepper

1. Peel the cucumber, cut into 5cm lengths and core out and discard the centres. Cut the cucumber pieces in half lengthways and then into half-moon pieces, each about 1cm in width. Put into a dish, sprinkle with the salt and leave for 40 minutes.

2. Mix the caster sugar with the boiling water, stir well and add the vinegar and then the dill and a grind of black pepper.

3. Wash the cucumber thoroughly and add it to the pickle mix. It will be ready to eat in about 3 hours.

Cullen skink

SERVES 4 PEOPLE

A leek, potato and smoked haddock in the finest tradition, borrowed from Morayshire in north-east Scotland where they tend to make it with onion rather than leeks. This is sturdy winter food and the quantities suggested make a dish suitable as a main course.

Pre-heat oven to 180C/gas mark 4

1. Cut the smoked haddock into 4-5 pieces and place in an ovenproof dish with the bay leaf. Pour half the milk over the top, cover the dish with tinfoil or a lid and bake in the oven for 30 minutes.

2. Peel the potatoes and chop into large dice. Steam until cooked. Warm the remaining milk and mash with the cooked potatoes and 25g butter – don't worry if the potato is a little chunky.

3. Now pour the fishy milk into the mashed potatoes and remove and discard the skin and bones from the fish. Add the chunks of haddock to the soup, together with ground black pepper and some salt – remembering the fish is quite salty.

4. Trim the leeks, cut into rings and steam.

5. Put all the ingredients in a pan with most of the chopped parsley and bring gently to simmering point on the stove. Serve in big bowls with a little extra parsley and a knob of butter to melt across the top.

450g smoked haddock

570ml/1pt milk

1 bay leaf

450g potatoes

3 leeks

bunch flat leaf parsley

50g butter

sea salt and black pepper

Endive, walnut and blue cheese salad

SERVES 4 PEOPLE AS A STARTER

Marriage of flavours sometimes sounds pretentious, but the tastes and textures in this attractive salad are superb. The vinaigrette is emulsified, tasty and quite chunky.

2 endives

250g St Agur cheese

12 fresh walnuts

2 ripe hass avocados

pumpkin seeds

Endives

1. Arrange 5 or 6 endive leaves on each plate and put nuggets of cheese and pieces of walnut in each leaf.

2. Peel, halve and dice the avocados and add, follow with a small scattering of pumpkin seeds. Spoon over a little vinaigrette over each leaf and serve.

vinaigrette

juice of a lemon

1 tsp Dijon mustard

3 tsp sugar

big pinch sea salt

125ml extra virgin olive oil

125ml sunflower oil

Vinaigrette (approximately 250ml)

Put the first four ingredients into a bowl and whisk vigorously, slowly adding first the olive oil followed by the sunflower oil. The net result should be well-emulsified vinaigrette that will keep for some days in the fridge and flavour many salads.

Focaccia bread

FOR 8 PEOPLE

Freezes well

Use a rectangular baking tray approx 18cm x 28 x 4cm. Line the bottom with baking parchment, oil the sides. Set oven to 230°/gas mark 8.

1. Sift the flours, yeast and sea salt into a large mixing bowl.

2. Stir in the malt extract or sugar into the warm water in a jug; add a tablespoon of olive oil.

3. Slowly pour the liquid into the flour mix and use dough hooks on the mixer or your hands to make well-kneaded, pliable dough. Put the dough into a clean bowl and cover with cling film; leave in a warm place until it has at least doubled in size.

4. Roll into a rectangle on a well-floured board and put it into the baking tray, making sure it goes into the corners (it should be very elastic at this stage). Cover again until the dough rises. Punch some holes in the top with your fingertip, sprinkle with sea salt, the chopped rosemary and splashes of olive oil. Cover and let it rise once more (minutes only). Bake for 10 minutes in the hot oven; then reduce the temperature to 200°C (gas mark 6) and bake for a further 10 minutes. Turn onto a cake rack.

50g plain flour

175g strong white flour

½ tsp Malvern salt or ground sea salt

1 level tsp dried yeast (Doves Farm is good)

6 fl ozs warm water

½ tsp malt extract or ½ tsp sugar

olive oil

2 sprigs rosemary, chopped

Gazpacho

SERVES 4 PEOPLE

Hola! Summer explodes from bowls of chilled gazpacho, fragrant with fresh tomato, green and red peppers, cucumber and garlic – trailed with a swirl of olive oil and served with crusty bread.

6 big ripe plum tomatoes

1 thick slice good white bread

½ cucumber

½ green pepper

½ red pepper

1 garlic clove

2 tbsp olive oil

1 tbsp vinegar

2 tbsp dry sherry

250mls iced water

salt and pepper

1. Slit the tomato skins, put in a bowl and cover with boiling water. Leave for a couple of minutes and run them under cold water. Slip the skins and pare out the green core at the top.

2. Cut the crusts from the bread, soak in a little cold water and break into chunks in the bottom of a bowl. Chop each tomato into big chunks and add to the bread.

3. Peel half the skin from the cucumber, cut into 2cm pieces and discard the seeds. Remove the seeds from the peppers and dice into similar size pieces. Peel the garlic clove and chop quite finely. Add all these ingredients to the bread and tomatoes.

4. Spoon in the olive oil, vinegar and sherry plus some salt and pepper.

5. Blend all the ingredients with 250mls iced water, and chill. Serve with a swirl of good olive oil in each bowl.

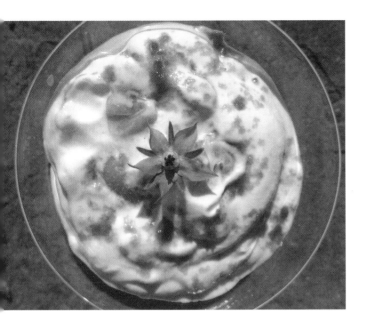

Gooseberry fool

SERVES 4 PEOPLE

It may sound ridiculous to use lemon juice as well as the sharp variety of green cooking gooseberries but the lemony addition to the whipping cream works wonders in making this the best of gooseberry fools – diaphanous in comparison to those made with double cream or custard!

1. Top, tail and wash the gooseberries, put into a pan with 3 tbsp of caster sugar and the water. Simmer gently until the fruit is soft, then mash with a fork until the fruit is just chunky. Once cool, refrigerate.

2. Whip the cream until it makes floppy peaks. Blend in the lemon zest and juice and chill. Just before serving, fold the gooseberries loosely into the cream, pile into dishes and top with a sprinkle of muscovado sugar.

350g green gooseberries

sugar

3 tbsp water

300ml whipping cream

zest and juice of ½ a lemon

dark brown muscovado sugar

Hollandaise sauce

SERVES 4 PEOPLE

Hollandaise in all its forms, with or without herbs, with or without a dab of Dijon mustard or just plain and simple – is the sauce that adds an immaculate finish to vegetables, notably asparagus or indeed new potatoes or baby carrots, as well as fish and meats. The inventor of Oeufs Bénédicte deserves special mention: what a combination. This version is thanks to Delia Smith. I've used all sorts of recipes, many of which work but are long-winded, some of which have a tendency to curdle. This is fast and easy and has never failed or curdled. Delia worries about keeping the Hollandaise warm but its impact with the appropriate food and when used at room temperature seems perfect to me – make it about an hour before serving.

2 egg yolks

1 tbsp fresh lemon juice

1 tbsp vinegar

100g unsalted butter

1 tsp freshly chopped chives or tarragon

1. Tip the egg yolks into a bowl or a small food blender and whiz.

2. Heat the lemon juice and vinegar until it begins to simmer, remove from the heat and pour slowly over the egg yolks whilst continuing to blend.

3. Melt the butter in a pan until bubbling. Remove from the heat and trickle into the Hollandaise mix, whisking or blending constantly. Add a little sea salt to taste and stir in the chives or tarragon.

Homity pies

MAKES 6-8 PIES

Quizzing food lovers in a bid to discover the provenance of homity pies has proved fruitless. What is certain is that they are simple to make and delicious.

Pre-heat the oven to 190°C/gas mark 5.
Use either little individual quiche tins or a tray for baking little cakes or tarts.

1. Make the pastry. Lightly oil the tart or cake tins and line with pastry.

2. Peel and finely chop the onion; cut the mushrooms into quarters. Heat the oil in a frying pan and soften the onion, add the mushrooms and cook for a further minute or two. Let it cool for 5 minutes before adding to the other ingredients.

3. Dice the potatoes into a large bowl; add the chopped parsley, cheese and the onion and mushroom mixture together with some seasoning. Fold the ingredients together and spoon into the pastry cases. Give each pie a dash of Worcester sauce and trickle cream over the top. Bake for 25 minutes and serve hot or cold.

pastry

150g plain flour

75g butter

pinch salt

iced water

filling

200g cooked potato

onion

mushroom

oil

parsley

cheese

Worcester sauce

salt and pepper

cream

Kholrabi, radish, pear and rocket salad with sesame dressing

SERVES 4 PEOPLE

So extraordinary are the sputnik-like arrangement of foliage and delicate pale green hue that kholrabi must have arrived on planet earth in a flying saucer. The flavour is something akin to the breakfast radish, mildly peppery and many agree that its delicacy is best tasted when the vegetable is raw. It mixes beautifully with radish and rocket but needs to be cut into very fine julienne; I'd advise using a mandolin for this but beware, mandolins mangle fingers. The sesame dressing goes well and the salad is a good match to Asian-style foods.

1 kholrabi

1 bunch radishes

50g rocket

1 conference pear

sesame seeds for toasting

dressing

3 tsp caster sugar

3 tsp white wine or cider vinegar

3 tsp soy sauce

3 tsp sesame seed oil

1. Top and tail and peel the kohlrabi, cut into juliennes. Wash the radishes and cut into thin rings. Peel the pear; use a potato peeler, cut into long strips.

2. Put a modest tablespoon of sesame seeds into a frying pan, toast until they begin to colour and pop in the pan.

3. Assemble the salad. Make the dressing by putting the sugar into a cup and adding a teaspoon of boiling water to dissolve. Add the rest of the ingredients and whisk with a fork. Sprinkle over the salad followed by a scattering of toasted sesame seeds. Serve immediately.

Leeks with egg and cress vinaigrette

SERVES 4 PEOPLE

Dressed with vinaigrette and chopped egg, the versatile leek is a delicious starter.

4 medium size leeks

vinaigrette

¼ tsp Dijon mustard

1 level tsp caster sugar

3 tbsp extra virgin olive oil

juice of ½ a lemon

salt and pepper

1 hard boiled egg

a box of mustard and cress

1. Trim the leeks, cut into lengths of approximately 10cms, split horizontally. Either steam or cook in a frying pan of boiling water until tender. Run carefully under cold water, drain, gently squeeze out the excess water and arrange on a plate.

2. Whisk the mustard, sugar, oil, lemon, salt and pepper together. Chop the boiled egg very finely and stir into the vinaigrette.

3. Spoon over the leeks and sprinkle with the mustard and cress.

Lemon posset

SERVES 4 PEOPLE

The quickest, easiest pudding in the world. Just don't be tempted to over cook the cream, and don't be alarmed at the moment when the lemon juice hits the cream in the saucepan and the whole lot appears to curdle.

1. Mix the sugar, cream and lemon zest in a pan and bring to simmering point whilst stirring constantly. Let it simmer gently for 2½ minutes.

2. Pour into ramekins or a dish and once the mixture is cold, set in the fridge for an hour or so.

   Serve alone or with a raspberry or blackberry purée.

300mls double cream

finely grated zest and the juice of a lemon

75g caster sugar

Lemon tart

SERVES 6 PEOPLE

I've tried lots recipes for tarte au citron, some too eggy, some too sharp, some too soggy, but this one seems to hit the mark. It is nicest made on the day, taken from the oven and left out of the fridge until required – with a dusting of icing sugar added at the last minute. The trick is to make the sweet pastry and blind-bake the case carefully until its crisp before adding the filling.

Preheat the oven to 180C/gas mark 4

1. Work the butter into the flour and icing sugar and add the iced water, a tablespoon at a time until the pastry is pliable. Wrap in cling film and chill for 30 minutes (it helps to stop the pastry cracking).

2. Line the bottom of a 25cm flan tin with baking parchment and butter the edges of the tin. Roll out the pastry to fit the tin and trim the edges. Now add another parchment circle on top of the pastry and fill the tin with clay baking balls or dried beans. Bake in the oven for 15 minutes, carefully remove the balls and parchment and return the pastry case to the oven for a further 15-20 minutes, until the edges of the pastry and browning. Remove from the oven.

3. Combine the eggs and sugar and whisk. Then add the cream, lemon juice and zest and whisk again. Pour into the flan case and bake for 25 minutes, until the top is just set.

Serve with crème fraîche, or fromage frais if you want the skinnier version.

sweet pastry

175g plain flour

1 tbsp icing sugar

100g soft, unsalted butter

2 tbsp cold water

filling

2 lemons (zest from one and juice from both)

3 eggs

100g caster sugar

100ml double cream

Marmalade

MAKES 8 X 1LB JARS

A steamy kitchen, a suffusion of orange – and finally a golden jelly suspending bright threads of peel – that's the aim. Marmalade-making is a ritual; the Seville oranges appear in the shops for a few weeks only at the beginning of the new year and although there are many short cuts proffered, I think the marmalade must be made with love and forethought – it's going to be looking at you on the breakfast table for the next twelve months. There are those who prefer chunky, brooding variety in the style of Coopers Old English; just cut the peel into sturdier pieces and cook for longer. Quantities and timings are approximate as the size of the pan and of the fruit is all part of the overall cooking equation.

I realise most of my recipes are in metric measurements, but this is the quirky exception – it is only perfect using these quantities!

1 kilo Seville oranges

4 pints water

4 lbs preserving sugar

1 lemon, squeezed

1. Wash the oranges. Halve and squeeze the juice from the fruit, reserving the pith and pips and pulling out any loose pith from the orange skins. Tie the pith and pips into a piece of muslin. Put the juice, muslin bag and water into a jam pan. Cut the orange-skin halves in half again, then slice very thinly across (rather than lengthways). Add to the pan. Bring to boil and simmer for 1-1½ hours until the liquid is reduced to about half. Remove the muslin and squeeze its juices back into the pan.

2. Add the sugar and lemon juice, stir until dissolved and boil for 25-30 minutes or until the marmalade will set on a cold plate. Allow it to settle until the tiny bubbles disappear. Pot in sterilized jars.

oranges are

MARMALA~

OT for snack

Medlar jelly

MAKES ABOUT FIVE 300ML JARS

Medlars are unprepossessing little fruits, like tiny Russet apples and when cut in half they resemble an apple in cross section. To enjoy a raw medlar, the fruit must be ripe, that's to say it looks brown and mushy, in medlar-speak, bletted. To eat raw, cut in half and scoop out the flesh.

Medlar jelly has the sharpness and cut of crab apple, but more flavour and it's perfect with meats such as lamb and pork or eaten by the spoonful on fresh bread or little pancakes with cream. There are plenty growing in the South West and they are around at the same time as the apple crop.

2 kilos medlars

4 lemons

8 cloves

granulated sugar

+ extra lemons

1. Wash the fruit, halve and put in a jam pan, add the lemons quartered. Just cover with water and add the cloves. Bring to the boil and cook the fruit until mushy, strain through a jelly bag into a large bowl. At this stage the liquid looks milky and frankly, slightly revolting.

2. Measure the liquid back into the jam pan and for every pint of juice, add a pound of sugar and a tablespoon of lemon juice. Bring to the boil, stirring until the sugar has dissolved. Begin to test the juice on a plate after 15 minutes and as soon as it shows signs of setting, turn off the heat. Skim the nasties from the surface and bottle in sterilized jars.

Mushroom and chive tart

SERVES 6 PEOPLE

Mushrooms may shrink on cooking, but their flavours intensify – and if it's the foraging season the varieties can be mixed to add yet more interesting flavours. The pastry-making might sound a slog but makes for a good crisp base.

These quantities are suitable for a 25cm (10") flan tin with removable bottom.

pastry

100g plain flour + 50g wholemeal flour

1 tbsp freshly-grated Parmesan

25g lard

50g butter

salt

2 tbsp iced water

The pastry

Preheat oven to 190C/gas mark 5

1. Cut 2 pieces of baking parchment to fit the base of the tin. Line the tin with one piece and butter around the edges of the tin. Mix the flours, Parmesan, lard, butter and salt in a food processor until it resembles fine crumbs. Add the water and blend rapidly until the pastry is pliable but not over mixed. Wrap in cling film and chill for 30 minutes.

2. Roll on a floury board and line the tin with the pastry and prick the bottom a few times with a fork. Cover the pastry base with the second piece of baking parchment and fill it with baking balls. Bake for 20 minutes. Carefully remove the balls and parchment and bake for a further 15 minutes or until pale golden.

The filling

Preheat the oven to 180C/gas mark 4

1. Slice the mushrooms. Heat the butter and olive oil and gently sauté the mushrooms until much of their liquid evaporates; season with the lemon juice and salt and pepper.

2. Whisk the eggs and cream together and add the Cheddar and chives. Scatter the mushrooms over the pastry base and pour over the creamy egg mix. Bake towards the top of the oven for 20-25 minutes, or until the top is just set. Serve warm.

filling

300g mushrooms

1 tsp butter

1 tbsp olive oil

juice of ¼ lemon

2 large eggs

200mls double cream

75g grated Cheddar

bunch of chives

sea salt and pepper

Boiled onions

SERVES 4 PEOPLE

Simple. Star food!

8 small to medium onions

water

salt and butter

1. Wash the onions in their skins and slice a tiny tranche from their bottoms so they will stand upright. Trim a similar piece from the top and make a shallow cross at the top of each onion.

2. Stand upright in a pan and add about an inch of water. Cover and simmer gently for 30 minutes or until the onions feel soft. Pop them from their skins and add a little butter and salt.

Parsnip crisps

SERVES 4 PEOPLE

These look and taste delicious with roasted game birds such as pheasant and partridge – and certainly with the Christmas turkey. Best served immediately but can be prepared a couple of hours in advance and warmed up at the last minute.

1. Peel the parsnips and use a mandolin to cut into thin rings.

2. Heat a sufficient depth of oil in a pan for the parsnips to be covered while they cook – approximately 4cm.

3. Once hot, fry a small handful at a time and when they are curly and slightly crisp, dry on kitchen roll and fry the next batch.

2 – 3 small or medium size parsnips

corn or sunflower oil

fine salt

Parsnip soup with pistou

SERVES 4-5 PEOPLE

Creamy, lightly curried winter soup spiked with a teaspoon of garlic pistou – the French answer to Italian pesto made with crushed basil leaves, garlic, olive oil and sea salt. In the absence of basil, flat-leaf parsley is a cracking substitute, and my preference in this particular soup.

3-4 parsnips – approx 650g

1 floury potato – approx 200g

25g butter

1 heaped tsp Sharwoods medium curry powder

1 litre chicken or veg stock

salt

4 tbsp double cream

pistou

small bunch basil or flat leaf parsley

1 garlic clove

pinch sea salt

2 tbsp olive oil

1. Peel and quarter the parsnips and cut out the woody cores. Chop into chunks. Peel the potato and chop into similar sized pieces. Steam the vegetables until cooked,

2. Melt the butter in a small pan, then stir in the curry powder and cook gently for a minute. Add 2-3 tablespoons of stock and stir well.

3. Warm the remainder of the stock and liquidize half-at-a-time with the vegetables. Return the purée to a saucepan, stir in the curry paste and heat gently. Add sea salt to taste and lastly the double cream.

4. Use a pestle and mortar to make the pistou. Tear the basil leaves or chop the parsley into small pieces, add a peeled, chopped garlic clove and the sea salt. Begin to crush the ingredients, gradually incorporating the olive oil. Swirl half a teaspoon into each soup bowl with a flick of extra cream.

Pear tarte Tatin

SERVES 6-8 PEOPLE

Pre-heat the oven to 220C/gas mark 7.

For the quantities listed here, use a tarte Tatin tin approximately 22cm in diameter.

1. Make the pastry in a food mixer. Cut the butter into the flour, icing sugar and salt, next add 2 tbsp iced water. Mix briefly until the pastry is pliable. Wrap in cling film and refrigerate for 20 minutes.

2. To make the tart, cover the bottom of the baking tin with half the butter, pushing it around with your fingers to spread if necessary – sprinkle on 2 tbsp of sugar.

3. Peel, core and cut the pears into halves and arrange tightly around the tin, rounded side down. Add the remaining tablespoon of sugar and dots of butter.

4. Roll out the pastry to cover the tin, trim around the edges and tuck the pastry down into the tin. Make a few fork holes in the top.

5. Bake for 30 minutes until the pastry is golden. If the pastry's browning too quickly turn down the oven a couple of notches. Leave in the tin for a further 30-40 minutes, then turn on to a plate.

Autumn's the time for making this tart, when fresh British Conference pears are plentiful. And make the pastry, it's a cinch. Nothing you can buy works as well for the base which is crisp like shortbread.

pastry

150g plain flour

75g butter

1 dessertspoon icing sugar

pinch salt

cold water, approx 2 tbsp

tarte

6-8 smallish Conference pears

3 tbsp light muscovado sugar

75g butter

Pickled pears

MAKES 2 x 500ml KILNER JARS

Serve with cheese and cold meats.
Ideal as part of a Boxing Day spread.

500ml cider vinegar

500g granulated sugar

1tsp allspice

1tsp whole cloves

2 small cinnamon sticks

zest of a small orange

6 small firm Conference pears

2 bay leaves

1. Pour the vinegar into a saucepan and stir in the sugar, bring to the boil and continue to stir until the sugar has dissolved. Add the allspice, cloves, cinnamon and orange zest and simmer for 5 minutes.

2. Peel and halve the pears. Add to the mixture and simmer for a further 10 minutes, turning occasionally. Lift the pears into sterilized jars. Boil the remaining mixture for a further 5 minutes, adding the bay leaf at the last minute. Pour over the pears, seal and store for about eight weeks before use.

Peas Madame Vibert

Peas with a classic French flair; their largesse of flavour and sweetness is especially good with white fish and meat.

25g butter

6 spring onions, trimmed and chopped

little gem lettuce, cut across into thin ribbons

250g shelled peas or mixture of peas and broad beans

2 tbsp double cream

1 tsp sugar

salt and pepper

(optional 1 tsp fresh chopped mint)

1. Soften the butter in the bottom of a pan, add the spring onions and soften slightly. Stir in the lettuce and cook gently for a further minute.

2. Add the peas, sugar and salt and barely cover with water. Simmer for about 15 minutes until the water has almost evaporated.

3. Stir in the cream, a little black pepper (and the mint if you've got it).

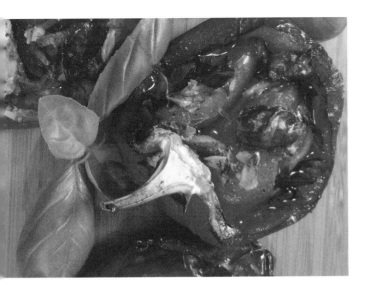

Piedmontese Peppers

STARTER FOR 4 PEOPLE

This is a perennial favourite, first brought to my attention by Delia Smith – delicious as a starter or main course.

Preheat oven to 180C/gas mark 4

1. Halve the peppers, scoop out the seeds and lay the peppers on a baking tray.

2. Slash the skins of the tomatoes, put into a basin and pour over boiling water. Leave for a minute, run under the cold tap and slip the skins from the tomatoes. Cut the fruits into quarters, putting 3 pieces into each pepper.

3. Roughly chop the anchovy fillets and sprinkle the centre of each pepper half with a fillet. Finely chop the garlic cloves and sprinkle over the peppers.

4. Add a little salt, some black pepper, a dessert-spoon of olive oil per pepper and a few torn basil leaves.

5. Roast for an hour or until the peppers are beginning to blacken around the edges. Add a little more basil and serve warm or cold, with all the juices.

2 biggish red peppers

3 plum tomatoes

½ tin anchovy fillets, drained

1 garlic clove, peeled

salt and pepper

olive oil

fresh basil

Bottled plums

MAKES 2 x 600ml/1 pint KILNER JARS

Each Kilner jar will hold 8-10 plums, depending on size. When the plums are in abundance in late summer, bottling seems a squirrel-like tactic but the pleasure of mid-winter crumble or plums and custard are just rewards. I have recently changed to using Kilner jars with disposable metal lids, very slightly more expensive but much easier to open.

Pre-heat oven to 150C/gas mark 2

1. Put new rubber rings on the jars; fill them with boiling water to sterilize. Chuck the water and stand jars on a wooden board.

2. Boil 600mls/1 pint of water and stir in the sugar, keep stirring until the sugar has dissolved.

3. Remove the stalks from the plums and wash the fruit in cold water. Pack loosely into the jars and pour over the syrup to within 2cm of the top.

4. Put a piece of newspaper on a baking tray and place the jars (with their metal clips in place but not locked down) on the tray. Bake on the top shelf of the oven for 45 minutes.

5. Bring the last of the syrup up to boiling point. Remove the jars to a wooden board and top up with the syrup. The jars will be scalding hot so use a cloth to save your hands and clip and seal them immediately.

6. Store in a dark, cool place. Unclip the metal seals, run under hot water for a minute or so and use a screw driver to ease open the lids. With the disposable tops – just stab and release the pressure.

1 kilo plums

225g granulated sugar

600ml/1 pint water

Warm new potato and smoked salmon salad with pickled cucumber and dill

SERVES 4 PEOPLE

After winter's long haul and an excess of ageing vegetables, welcome to the pleasure of waxy new potatoes, so young and fresh their skins rub away with the lightest touch. This recipe is potato salad with knobs on, not at all slimming. For the pickled cucumber I use either the pickled recipe on page 30, or the sort that comes in large jars.

450g new potatoes

3 tbsp mayonnaise

1 tsp milk

1 tsp grainey mustard

2 tsp fresh, finely chopped dill

2 pickled cucumbers, cut into rings

200g smoked salmon, cut into strips

lemon wedge

sea salt and black pepper

1. Scrub and either steam or boil the new potatoes until tender. Let them cool and remove their skins, then dice and season with salt and pepper

2. Stir a smidgeon of milk into the mayonnaise to thin it a little. Mix together the mustard, mayonnaise and dill and cut the salmon into strips about 2cm wide.

3. Cut the cucumber into rings and fold all the ingredients together.

Serve on dressed lettuce leaves with a squeeze of lemon.

Pumpkin and ginger soup

SERVES 4 PEOPLE

I've tried to like sweet pumpkin pie but no luck so far. However this soup has quite the reverse effect on my taste buds, it's delicious.

Preheat the oven to 190C/gas mark 5

1. Using a big knife or kitchen cleaver, halve the pumpkin and chop that half into medium-size chunks – cut away the seeds. Paint the chunks with vegetable oil, place them on a baking tray and roast for approximately 45 minutes or until the flesh is soft.

2. Remove from the oven and scoop the roasted flesh from the pumpkin skin. Using a coarse grater, grate about 2-3cms of fresh ginger. Liquidize the pumpkin, stock and ginger with the crème fraîche.

3. Reheat the soup to serve, sprinkle with freshly chopped parsley.

½ a medium pumpkin

1 piece fresh ginger

sunflower oil

750ml vegetable or chicken stock

1 tbsp crème fraîche

Radishes with anchovy dip

A summer snack to accompany glasses of rosé, cider or perry, or as part of a cold table. Radishes vary from the mild red and white breakfast radish to small, peppery and hot red ones – and to the very handsome heritage varieties.

2 bunches of radishes

200g mayonnaise

4-5 anchovies

½ tsp capers

½ tsp Dijon mustard

1. Trim and wash the radishes.

2. Blend the other four ingredients to make a delectable dip.

Raspberry no-churn ice cream

SERVES 6 PEOPLE

A cunning ploy that uses condensed milk rather than a custard in the ingredients, thus dispensing with an ice cream maker. Kirsch is a good spirit for outing the flavours of many fruits and it helps prevent the ice cream from over-freezing.

1. Put the raspberries in a small pan with the caster sugar and the tiniest splash of water to prevent the sugar burning. Bring to simmering point and cook for a couple of minutes. Rub through a sieve; stir the kirsch into the purée. Refrigerate.

2. Whip the double cream and condensed milk until it begins to form soft peaks. Put in the freezer for an hour.

3. Fold in the raspberry purée but try not to over-mix; it looks much prettier if the streaky effect is maintained. Freeze for a minimum of a further 3 hours before serving.

Remove from the freezer 30 minutes before serving or put in the microwave for 1 minute on defrost; delicious with fresh raspberries.

200g fresh raspberries

2 tsp caster sugar

1 tbsp kirsch

300mls double cream

200g (approx ½ tin) condensed milk

Ratatouille

SERVES 4 PEOPLE

Robust Mediterranean vegetable stew that packs a punch with grilled or roasted food – and it tastes just as good eaten hot or cold. Alternatively serve as a starter with crusty bread to mop up the juices.

1. Heat half the oil and begin by frying the onion until soft. Follow this with the aubergine and fry until the outside colours. Put into an ovenproof dish.

2. Add more oil to the frying pan and fry the rest of the vegetables just to the point where they begin to soften and colour. Sprinkle with a couple of pinches of sea salt and add some black pepper. Stir all the vegetables into the ovenproof dish, cover with a lid or tinfoil and put in a medium oven for 15 minutes. Serve warm or cold.

3-4 tbsp olive or sunflower oil

1 onion, peeled and sliced

1 medium aubergine, diced

3 tomatoes, chopped

3-4 courgettes, cut into rings about 2cm thick

1 red pepper, de-seeded and cut into chunks

1-2 garlic cloves, peeled and finely chopped

sea salt and black pepper

Red cabbage

SERVES 6 PEOPLE

Pre-heat oven to 190C/ gas mark 5

750g red cabbage, thinly sliced

1. Layer the cabbage, onion and apple alternately in the pot. When completing each layer, sprinkle with 1 tsp sugar and some salt and pepper.

1 onion, peeled and thinly sliced

1 bramley apple, peeled, cored and sliced

2. Spoon over the olive oil and wine, cover and bake in the centre of the oven for 75-90 minutes.

soft brown sugar

1 tbsp olive oil

Once cooked, this baked red cabbage can be kept in the fridge for a day or two and then reheated.

3 tbsp red wine or 2 tbsp red wine vinegar

As well as being traditional with Christmas turkey, it's also delicious with roast pork and duck.

salt and pepper

Red onion marmalade

MAKES 1 LB JAR

Eat spoonfuls with coarse pâtés, terrines, cold meats and some cheeses – make it a feature on a cold buffet table. I use half-and-half olive and sunflower oil and just a little chilli not to drown other flavours.

1. Peel and thinly slice the onions and sauté gently in the oil until soft.

2. Add the remaining ingredients and simmer, uncovered, for about an hour, stirring from time to time.

3. Store in the fridge when cold: it keeps for two to three weeks.

3 red onions

3 tbsp olive oil or sunflower oil

175ml red wine

125ml red wine vinegar

100g light brown muscovado sugar

(optional ½ chilli, de-seeded and chopped)

salt and pepper

Pink sparkling rhubarb jelly

SERVES 6 PEOPLE

A spring frivolity to celebrate the early rhubarb from the Yorkshire Triangle; the latter is the heartland for the first English rhubarb of the season. The delicate flavour and fine pink stalks earn it the nickname of champagne rhubarb.

400mls rosé wine

350g young rhubarb

100g caster sugar

150ml can soda water, chilled

1 sachet gelatine (sufficient for 500mls liquid)

1. Top and tail the rhubarb and cut into 2cm lengths.

2. Pour 200mls wine into a saucepan over a medium heat, add the caster sugar and stir until dissolved. Now add the rhubarb, bring to simmering point and cook for a couple of minutes, until soft. Pour carefully into a dish to cool, then refrigerate for an hour or so.

3. To make the jelly, put half the remaining wine in a small bowl and sprinkle over the gelatine. Leave for 10 minutes.

4. Heat the last of the wine in a pan and bring it to simmering point, add the gelatine mixture, stir well until the gelatine has dissolved but don't let it boil. Remove from the heat and pour into the rhubarb with the can of soda water.

5. Spoon into individual moulds or a large jelly mould and leave in the fridge to set for 4-5 hours.

Serve with cream.

YORKSHIRE

Roasted vegetables

SERVES 4 PEOPLE

Comfort food for cold days, a choice of flavours with fish, meat or game – and a sharing dish with barbecued food. I leave potatoes out of the equation, but here are the quantities used in the photograph, plenty for four.

Heat the oven to 220C/gas mark 7.

1. Scrub the carrots and cut away their green tops. Peel the parsnip, cut out its woody centre and cut into chunks. Quarter the red pepper, de-seed and cut into medium strips. Peel and quarter the red onions. Trim the top of the fennel and cut into 1cm slices. Top and tail the courgettes and cut into pieces.

2. Put a little oil in a roasting tin and put it in the oven to heat. Steam the vegetables in 2 batches for about 5 minutes each batch; this just begins to soften the vegetables and means they go into the oven already hot.

3. Put all vegetables in roasting tin. Sprinkle a couple of tablespoons of olive oil over the top and add sea salt and black pepper. Roast for 45 minutes.

4. Add either oregano, chopped parsley or a little chopped fennel feather. Roast for a further 15 minutes or until the vegetables are beginning to go golden at the edges.

8 Chantenay carrots or 2 largish carrots chopped

1 parsnip

1 red pepper

2 red onions

1 large fennel bulb

2 courgettes

sea salt and black pepper

fresh oregano

olive oil

Somerset Cider Brandy pudding with blackberry

SERVES 6 PEOPLE

This may be smarty-pants blackberry and apple but it's light and utterly delicious. To make it properly the cream needs be the whipping variety rather than double and the apples should be cooked with their skins on in order to achieve a big depth of flavour – Somerset Cider Brandy or Calvados are magisterial additions.

500-550g Bramley apples

juice of ½ lemon

150mls water

caster sugar

300ml whipping cream

2 tbsp Somerset Cider Brandy or Calvados or kirsch

200g blackberries

1. Wash the apples, cut any rotten bits and chop each into eights. Put into a pan with the lemon juice, water and 2 tbsp of caster sugar. Cover the pan and simmer gently until the apple is soft and fluffy, making sure the sugar doesn't burn. Rub the fruit through a sieve and leave the purée to cool.

2. Whip the cream into soft folds, incorporating a tablespoon of caster sugar. Stir in the Cider Brandy or Calvados. Now fold in the apple in swirls so there are visible streaks of green purée.

Serve with blackberry purée: 200g blackberries cooked with a tablespoon of water and a tablespoon of caster sugar until soft. Rub through a sieve and chill.

Spinach and cheese pies

SERVES 4 PEOPLE

This dish can be the richer for the addition of a chopped shallot, softened by frying in a little oil or butter and added to the spinach and cheese mixture.

Preheat the oven to 220C/gas mark 7

1 packet filo pastry

500g fresh spinach

50g Cheddar cheese, grated

50g Gruyère cheese, grated

25g melted unsalted butter

salt, pepper and nutmeg

1. Trim and discard the stems from the spinach and wash the leaves. Steam or boil the leaves, drain well and when sufficiently cool, press out the excess water.

2. Mix with the grated cheeses and add a little salt, some nutmeg and black pepper (plus the optional cooked shallot)

3. Cut 12 pieces of filo pastry, approximately 10cm x 10cm in order to use 3 squares for each spinach parcel. Arrange each set of 3 pieces in star shapes, one piece on top of another and spoon ¼ of the spinach mixture on each set.

4. Using a pastry brush, pile up the filo around the spinach, painting the outside of each layer with butter as you go.

5. Bake for 10-15 minutes until golden.

Spinach roulade

MAKES 8-10 PORTIONS

This roulade gathers flavour momentum if made in advance, ideally the day before, and left overnight in the fridge. Fresh spinach is essential; the fillings can be smoked salmon, cream cheese and finely chopped celery, taramasalata or whatever fires your taste buds.

4 eggs

200g well drained, cooked spinach (400g fresh spinach)

1 level tbsp freshly-grated Parmesan

50g soft butter

nutmeg

salt and black pepper

170g taramasalata

Pre-eat oven to 190C/gas mark 5

1. Butter a sheet of baking parchment and line a swiss roll tin approx. 32 x 24cms.

2. Separate the eggs. Put the cooked spinach, egg yolks, Parmesan cheese, butter, a little freshly-grated nutmeg and some salt and pepper into a food processor and mix together.

3. Beat the egg whites and fold gently but very thoroughly into the spinach mixture. Spoon into the baking tin, making sure the mixture reaches the corners, bake for 10 minutes and let the roulade cool for up to an hour in the tin.

4. Cut the roulade in half across the tin width and turn each half, top side down, on to cling film on a board. Spread the taramasalata on to each half and then roll each one lengthways to make 2 roulades. Put them on a plate, wrapped in their cling film and refrigerate. Slice just before serving.

Attractive if one half of the roulade is filled with taramasalata and the other half with smoked salmon.

Strawberries: an Eton Mess

SERVES 6 PEOPLE

The invention of Eton Mess must have been the consequence of a schoolboy lark with a bowl of meringues, strawberries and cream. However, apart from plucking warm fruit from the plant and eating it on the spot, I think it's the most sybaritic way of enjoying the strawberries.

1. Put 200g of the strawberries into a liquidiser with 2 tsp of sugar and whizz to make a purée.

2. Whip the cream until it flops in folds, add 2 tsp of sugar and the brandy. Whip a little more until the brandy incorporates into the cream.

3. An hour before pudding time, cut up the remaining strawberries and sprinkle with 2 tsp of sugar.

4. Just before serving, crumble 8 meringues into the cream, fold in the strawberry pieces and trickle a little of the purée over the top. Use the remainder to pour on each portion.

500g strawberries

6 tsp caster sugar

284ml whipping cream

2 tbsp Somerset Cider Brandy

8 meringues

meringues

2 egg whites

100g caster sugar

To make meringues

Preheat oven to 140C/gas mark 1

1. Whip the egg whites into peaks, gradually adding the sugar. Spoon the meringues on to baking parchment on a baking tray and cook for an hour.

2. Turn upside down and return to the oven for a further 15 minutes.

Sweetcorn chowder

SERVES 4 PEOPLE

Chowders are boisterous vegetable soups, often containing fish; this Thai-style version of chowder lends itself well to the addition of chicken, prawns – and even white crab meat or crab claws.

1 litre chicken stock

a large potato, about 300g

1 onion

1 garlic clove

1 jalapeño chilli

1 red pepper

2 tbsp vegetable oil

3 sweetcorn cobs

4 chicken thighs, skinned

(optional 12 prawns)

160g can of coconut cream

salt

tbsp chopped coriander

1. Pour the chicken stock into a large pan. Peel and dice the potato, add to the stock, cover the pan and cook until soft. Use a potato masher to break down the cooked potato cubes.

2. Peel and chop the onion and garlic. Remove any seeds from the chilli and chop very finely. Take out the seeds from the pepper and cut into thin slices. Strip the corn cobs of their foliage and cut down the sides to remove the kernels.

3. Heat the oil and in a separate pan, gently fry the onion until it begins to soften; add the garlic, chilli and red pepper. Stir into the chicken and potato stock with the corn kernels and chicken thighs – cover and simmer gently for about 40 minutes. If adding prawns now is the time to throw them into the pot. Stir in the coconut milk (or a couple of tablespoons of double cream) and taste the soup, adding salt if necessary. Serve with a sprinkling of fresh coriander.

Tartiflette
potato, onion
and bacon pie

SERVES 4 PEOPLE

Traditionally a dish from the Haute-Savoie in the French Alps, tartiflette is an irre-sistible one for a cold day. If following its French ethnicity, then use the wonderful rich and creamy Reblochon cheese from the region. I use mature Cheddar. Better older floury potatoes than new waxy ones.

Pre-heat oven to 190C/gas mark 5

1. Peel and finely chop the onion. Heat the oil in a frying pan and begin to soften the onion, add the bacon and thyme and continue to cook until the fat runs from the bacon.

2. Peel and slice the potatoes to about ½ cm thick; wash in cold water and drain. Bring a large pan of water with a level teaspoon of salt to boiling point and add the sliced potatoes – simmer for 8-12 minutes until cooked but not falling apart. Empty carefully into a colander.

3. Grate the Cheddar or slice the Reblochon. Oil a shallow ovenproof dish and layer with potato, the onion and bacon, cheese and crème fraîche – finishing with potato, a sprinkling of cheese and a little black pepper

4. Bake for 45 minutes or until the tartiflette smells glorious and is bubbling in its dish.

Serve with salad or simply cooked white meat or fish.

Ingredients
1 medium onion
1 tbsp olive or sunflower oil
100g smoked streaky bacon or bacon lardons
½ tsp fresh thyme
600-700g potatoes
1 generous tbsp crème fraîche
100g mature Cheddar or Reblochon
salt and pepper

Tomato tarts with thyme, basil and goat's cheese

A STARTER FOR 8 PEOPLE, MAIN COURSE FOR 4

Almost the simplest, quickest of starters in kitchen
history, but the all-butter puff pastry is imperative.
Choose really flavoursome tomatoes and use a
large pastry cutter, about 10cm in diameter.

375g pack of Jus-Rol all butter
puff pastry

6-8 ripe tomatoes

150g goat cheese

bunch of fresh lemon thyme,
leaves stripped from stalks

fresh basil

caster sugar

olive oil

salt and pepper

Pre-heat the oven to 220C/gas mark 7

1. Roll out the pastry until quite thin and cut 8-10
   circles. Lift the pastry on to a lightly oiled baking
   tray; slice the tomatoes thinly and put about 3
   slices on each piece of pastry.

2. Scatter crumbled goat cheese over each tart,
   followed by the lemon thyme and some basil
   leaves.

3. Sprinkle each with a pinch of sugar; add freshly
   ground salt and pepper and splash liberally with
   extra virgin olive oil.

4. Bake for 20 minutes or until the pastry is golden.

   Serve warm. Chilled Manzanilla sherry is a great
   accompaniment.

Wallace and Gromit's beetroot salad

SERVES 4 PEOPLE

Made with lovely crumbly Wensleydale cheese and go-faster rocket.

50g rocket

1-2 cooked beetroot

8 fresh walnuts

100g Wensleydale cheese

fine zest of an orange

walnut oil

balsamic vinegar

sea salt and black pepper

1. Scatter some rocket on each plate. Peel and dice the beetroot and crack the fresh walnuts. Sprinkle over the beetroot, together with the crumbled Wensleydale cheese.

2. Now add the zest of a finely grated orange to the beetroot pieces and zigzag the salad with plenty of walnut oil and a splash of balsamic vinegar. Season with a little sea salt and black pepper.

Watercress mousse

serves 6 people

The best months for watercress are May until November and it's packed with all sorts of things that purport to be good for you. Serve with toast and butter – or smoked salmon, prawns or cold poached trout.

1. Put 3 tbsp stock into a bowl and sprinkle with the gelatine.

2. Heat the oil and soften the onion for 2 minutes. Roughly chop the watercress. Add to the pan; cover and soften for a further 3 minutes, turning a few times. Pour in the stock and bring to simmering point. Turn off the heat and stir the dissolved gelatine into the hot mixture.

3. Liquidize everything with the crème fraîche. Taste to check the seasoning; depending on the stock, it probably needs a little salt and pepper. Pour into a bowl and move to the fridge when cold.

4. Once the mousse begins to set around the edges, whisk the egg whites and fold into the mixture.

5. Spoon into a loaf tin, china bowl or ramekins and leave for several hours in the fridge to set. Dip into warm water to turn out the mousse.

350ml stock

1 packet gelatine, sufficient to set 500mls of liquid

1 small onion or 2 shallots, peeled and finely chopped

1 tbsp sunflower or veg oil

2 bunches watercress, ends of stems cut off and discarded

2 tbsp crème fraîche

salt and pepper

2 egg whites

Watercress sauce

SERVES 4 PEOPLE

Delicious, nutritious – and fantastic
with chicken or fish.

big bunch watercress

1 shallot or small onion

1 tbsp sunflower or corn oil

150ml sunflower or vegetable
stock

2 tbsp crème fraîche

sea salt and black pepper

1. Trim the end of the stem from the watercress and
   discard; roughly chop the rest of the bunch.

2. Peel and finely chop the shallot or onion. Heat the
   oil in a saucepan or wok and soften the shallot over
   a low heat. Stir in the watercress and continue to
   cook gently for a couple of minutes until the leaves
   soften.

3. Add the vegetable stock and bring to simmering
   point. Pour the watercress and stock into a liquidizer and add the crème fraîche – whiz until smooth.

4. Pour back into the saucepan and simmer for a
   couple of minutes to thicken the sauce. Check the
   seasoning as it may need a little salt. Serve with
   fish or chicken.

Windy city soup

SERVES 4 PEOPLE

Addictive! But avoid socially sensitive situations for an hour or so after.

1. Scrub the artichokes and peel off any very earthy bits; chop each into quarters. Pour the chicken stock into a pan, add the cleaned artichokes and simmer for 10 minutes or until soft.

2. Blitz in a liquidizer and sieve into a basin. Stir in 2 good pinches of sea salt, some ground black pepper and 3 tbsp of double cream.

   Serve with a little swirl of cream, a grind of the pepper mill and a sprinkle of parsley.

   Fried parsley

   Frying parsley turns it a lovely dark, crisp green. Chop a small bunch of parsley, heat a tablespoon of vegetable oil, fry quickly, drain on kitchen roll and sprinkle on the soup.

8 Jerusalem artichokes

750ml chicken stock

sea salt and black pepper

3 tbsp double cream

(optional 1 tbsp fried parsley)

Fruit and vegetables

APRICOT **Apricot chutney p10** Plump fresh apricots are in the shops in July and August.

ARTICHOKE, GLOBE Snap off the thick stem just below the head. Cover in water and simmer for approximately 45 minutes until the leaves pull away easily. Drain upside-down. Serve with vinaigrette. July, August and September.

ARTICHOKE, JERUSALEM **Windy City soup p87** Winter food.

APPLE, COOKING **Somerset cider brandy pudding p76** Autumn.

APPLE, EATING **Apple fritters in cider batter p8** Autumn brings a deluge of magnificent UK fruit.

ASPARAGUS **Risotto p11, Tart p12** To prepare and cook simply, wash the asparagus and cut off the woody ends of the stems. Steam for approximately 8-10 minutes, depending on the thickness of the stems. Serve either with butter and sea salt or with Hollandaise sauce, mayonnaise or shavings of Gruyère or Manchego cheese. Best of season April to the end of June, traditionally the 21st – midsummer night.

AVOCADO **Endive, walnut and blue cheese salad p34** Hass avocados with the knobbly skin are nicest; ripe when their skin darkens.

AUBERGINE **Thyme-baked with olive oil p14, Ratatouille p69**

BANANA Make banana bread or try mashed banana with brown sugar, cream and a drop of rum.

BEANS, BROAD **Risotto p11** Buy while the beans inside their furry pods are still small, steam or boil for a short time and serve with butter, sea salt and pepper – luxury spring fare. Once the skins around the beans toughen, you have the tedious task of popping each out of its overcoat before cooking.

BEANS, RUNNER. Buy while young, skim the strings from the edges and thinly slice. Steam or boil and serve with butter, sea salt and pepper.

BEANS, FRENCH Snap off the tips, steam or boil, serve with a little olive oil, crushed garlic and seasoning.

BEETROOT **Beetroot jelly p16, Wallace and Gromit's salad p84**

BLACKBERRIES **Somerset cider brandy pudding p76** Make wild, silky-textured bramble jelly with intense flavour, unobtainable from cultured berries. August and September for wild blackberries – after which the witches are said to debase them!

BLACKCURRANTS Essential for summer pudding. Freeze well. Make cheerful and healthy winter jelly. June and July.

BLUEBERRIES Eat raw in fruit salads. Summer.

BROCCOLI Steamed, or puréed to make Broccoli and Stilton soup.

BRUSSEL SPROUTS It would be a winter blessing to feel more charitable about sprouts, or indeed to have an artful ways of cooking them. The very small ones right at the top of the stem are best, and preferably home-grown. My mother used to tell me that eating sprouts was like being a giant eating cabbages; I remain unconverted.

CABBAGE Steam, or if the cabbage is crisp and sweet, shred finely and use in salad. Love the pointed Hispi cabbages cut across into slices, steamed and served with butter and seasoning. Colcannon, alias Bubble-and-Squeak, remains firm favourite for leftovers. You need cooked mashed potato, cabbage, an onion, some butter or meat dripping and seasoning. Peel, slice and soften the onion, add half the cabbage and potato and fry until the bottom is crisping, turn over and add the remaining ingredients. Keep going until the crisp bits mingle through the ingredients.

CABBAGE, RED **the classic recipe p70**

CARROTS Like broad beans, most delicious in their prime when young and the cooking time is minimal. Just add butter and parsley or chives. An excellent vegetable cut into julienne and eaten raw in salads, made into carrot and parsley soup or added to casseroles to give sweetness and flavour. But they don't help you to see in the dark; this was WW2 propaganda to persuade the Germans that our pilots could see at night (in fact we were using radar).

CAULIFLOWER Steamed, soups – particularly the luscious French Crème Dubarry, cauliflower cheese, spiced cauliflower.

CELERIAC **Celeriac soup p21** Funny, knobbly, celery-flavoured root vegetable – often left out in the cold as its looks are unpromising. However it's one of the best root vegetables for mashing; use half-and-half potato and celeriac. Serve with butter, nutmeg, seasoning and a fistful of chopped flat leaf parsley stirred in at the last minute.

CELERY **Braised celery p20, Celery, tomato and echalion sauce p24**

CHARD Cut out the stalks, then treat like fresh spinach; steam or boil, drain well, add salt, butter and some nutmeg.

CHERRIES Watch for the ripe and beautiful fruits from UK, USA and Hungary in mid-summer, large and luscious.

CHICORY Years ago chicory was sold whole, and looked as exotic as Mrs Schilling's Ascot millinery. Nowadays it tends to come in snapped-off portions in a bag of mixed salad. Hey ho, times change.

CHILLI See HERBS. All strengths available; ask advice before over-heating a dish. Green jalapeños strike a happy medium.

COURGETTE **Frittata p27, Ratatouille p69**
The most versatile of vegetables. Can be eaten raw, stuffed, fried, boiled, pureed and spiced.

CRESS Buy it! It has a beautiful smell and adds delicate flavour to salads. Tea-time egg sandwiches would be unthinkable without it.

CRANBERRY Cranberry sauce with turkey.

CUCUMBER **Braised cucumber with chives p28, Cucumber and yoghurt soup p29, Danish pickled cucumber p30**

DATES Big fat fresh dates, dates stuffed with walnuts or marzipan, dates in cakes – or dates eaten with Cheddar cheese and nuts. All delicious.

EDAMAME BEANS *alias* soya beans. Upped their profile in recent times in the UK. Look like peas. Boil for 5 minutes in lightly-salted water and pop from their shells. Healthy looking, bright green and great in salads.

ENDIVE **Endive, walnut and blue cheese salad p34** Braised endive is a great vegetable with fish. Cut in half and steam for 5 minutes, toss into a little hot oil or butter in a frying pan, add sea salt and serve when the edges are golden.

FENNEL Fennel's aniseed flavours work wonders with fish. Cut in thin strips for salad or braise as above with endive. Add a little fine orange zest for extra interest.

FIG I have a fig tree in the garden, a variety called Brown Turkey, well adapted to life in a UK climate. They ripen beautifully and we eat them cut into quarters with a splash of brandy and some cream.

GARLIC Don't use garlic if it's soft or discoloured and don't let it burn. Whilst headily appetizing when crisp and young, it taints food when stale.

GINGER A versatile rhizome that adds potency to spiced dishes or can be used in drinks and sweet food – fresh ginger, lemon and honey is a good adversary for a cold, or at very least it gives that impression. Use the roots while still fresh and juicy; peel and grate – or slice thinly into drinks.

HORSERADISH A pungent root and part of the Brassicaceae family. To make horseradish sauce, wash and peel about 20cm of root, pulverize with a couple of tablespoons of water, strain and add a tablespoon of white wine vinegar. Stir in a little lightly whipped cream before serving. Beware its ferocity!

ICEBERG LETTUCE Finest lettuce for a hot day. As its name suggests, it's good chilled, cut into wedges and served with a simple blue cheese dressing.

JERUSALEM ARTICHOKE, see ARTICHOKE

KALE My sentiments about kale are similar to sprouts, a personal struggle to raise enthusiasm. Kale looks so attractive but it is a chewy business wading through even the most discreet portion. Sorry Kale.

KIWI FRUIT It's good for you! Lots of vitamin C and potassium; peel and chop into fruit salads or green salads. Cooking destroys the vitamins.

KHOLRABI Kholrabi, radish and pear salad p42 A weird and wonderful looking sci-fi vegetable, similar to mild radish in flavour.

LEEK Leeks with egg and cress vinaigrette, p44 No Burns Night menu would forgo its cauldron of Cock-a-Leekie soup – chicken stock, leek and potato with plenty of salt and black pepper.

LEMON Lemon posset p45 I have just been introduced to the fragrance of the Sorrento lemon in our local Italian deli, Divino; a large and beautiful specimen lay on the counter for all to inhale and admire. As with oranges, the skins contain the oils and a fine zest of lemon will infuse a whole dish.

LETTUCE Peas Madame Vibert's p60 Bags of choice. Round, curly, red, bitter, sweet – all noticeably improved by a 30-minute dunk in cold water before draining and drying on kitchen paper. Contain useful amounts of potassium and vitamin A.

LIME Fresh lime juice squeezed over slices of mango or pawpaw; alternatively liquidize a peeled mango with juice of a lime and a little cream, chill and serve with a sprig of fresh mint.

LOGANBERRY A fruit related more to the blackberry than the raspberry, despite its ruby hue.

MANGELWURZEL No serious suggestions for such a lovely sounding object that is used mainly for animal fodder.

MANGETOUT *alias* snow peas are a flat-podded variety of pea. Zip off the stringy sides and blanch or stir-fry.

MANGO Delicious fruit with a big flat stone in the centre from which slices of golden flesh can be cut. Eat in fruit salad or very simply, with a good squeeze of fresh lime juice squeezed over the top. When puréed with the lime and a little cream, it looks like a glorious yellow custard. Serve chilled.

MEDLAR Medlar jelly p50

MELON You need a good nose and a good thumb to buy melon at its best. Gently press the top of the softer skin varieties to feel for any give – also smell the skins to see if you can catch a waft of honeyed ripeness. When really ripe, Honeydews are mouthwateringly good. Thread chunks of several varieties on to skewers for summer buffets.

MUSHROOM Chanterelle mushrooms with scrambled egg p25, Mushroom and chive tart p52 Be adventurous, but only in the hands of a professional forager.

NECTARINES. Delicious new varieties around including the Doughnut nectarine and peach, squat fruits shaped like a ring doughnut. The flavours are mouth-watering and they seem to ripen easily.

NUTS Chestnut stuffing p26 Autumn is the season heralded by green Kentish Cobnuts with walnuts and sweet chestnuts following on.

ORANGES Candied chocolate orange peel p17, Caramelized oranges p18, Marmalade p48

ONION Boiled onions in their skins p54 No disputing the general versatility of the onion. Red onions keep well and tend to be a little sweeter; if using them in salads blanch in boiling water and then run under a cold tap: it removes the overbearing sting of raw onion.

PAPAYA Peel, scoop out the black seeds, slice the fruit into fruit salad or better still, eat with a big squeeze of fresh lime juice.

PARSNIP **Parsnip crisps p55, Parsnip soup p56, Roasted vegetables p75**

PEACH One of the fruits that will tell you when it's ripe by the fragrance. Try the sumptuous new dough-nut-shaped varieties that seem to manage to combine all the desirable elements of a peach.

PEAR **Pear tarte Tatin p57, Pickled pear p58** Many luscious varieties for eating fresh, but for me, firm Conference pears are tops for cooking, retaining their texture and flavour.

PEAS **Peas Madame Vibert p60**

PEPPER **Piedmontese peppers p61**

PLUM **Bottled plums p63** The quality and versatility of Victoria plums is hard to beat.

POMEGRANATE in **Aubergine thyme-baked p14**

POTATO **Warm new potato and smoked salmon salad p64, Tartiflette p81** Choose potatoes carefully, both for flavour and texture; floury varieties for roasting, waxy varieties for steaming or salads. Don't use green potatoes, they contain solanine, a poison that will upset the gut.

PUMPKIN **Pumpkin and Ginger Soup p65** Good for hollowing out and a giving a toothy grin at Halloween.

QUINCE Makes excellent slightly gritty-textured jelly to eat on scones or ladle into apple pie to give a dimension beyond expectation.

RADICCHIO Red leaf chicory with large white veins, looks like a mini round lettuce and has a pleasant bitter tang when used in salads.

RADISH **Radish with anchovy dip p66** Another member of the extensive *Brassicaceae* family, peppery crisp in flavour. Long Breakfast radishes with the white splash at the root are milder; goodness knows why they're called breakfast radish. All varieties make an excellent snack tickled up with a grain or two of sea-salt or chopped into salad.

RASPBERRY **Raspberry no-churn ice cream p67** Best of the summer soft fruit; puréed raspberry adds delicious zing to lots of fruits – and marries well with chocolate puddings too.

RED CURRANT Ripening hand-in-hand with black-currants in early to mid summer; this little jewelled berry makes the jelly that is so traditional with roast lamb or some game dishes. Stir a spoonful into lamb and game gravy to add piquancy.

RHUBARB **Pink sparkling rhubarb jelly p72** The first rhubarb of the year pre-empts most of other new season's fruit and vegetables, appearing in the shops in very early spring from the W Yorkshire Triangle. Its pale pink hue and delicacy justify its nickname, Champagne Rhubarb.

SALSIFY A long tapering root vegetable that looks like a dandelion root and is indeed related. Scrub off its muddy coating, peel to reveal the white flesh (easiest done with a potato peeler), and cut into short lengths – at which point it feels slightly glutinous; boil gently in acidulated water for about 45 minutes or until tender. A teaspoonful of lemon juice or white wine vinegar in the water will give the necessary acidity. Serve with butter and salt.

SAMPHIRE *alias* Sea Asparagus, and found in mid-summer in some of our home waters, particularly in the estuaries on the Norfolk coast. Although available in other months, nothing matches the salt-infused succulence of the real McCoy. Snap off any root or woody ends, wash well in fresh water and boil or steam until tender. Serve with butter, either as an accompaniment to dish to fish or lamb – or as a starter.

SHALLOT Related to but milder and sweeter than the onion. The 'banana' shallots, *aka* echalions, are particularly easy to peel and chop, and have an excellent flavour. They carry less moisture than the onion so cook slowly to avoid burning. The Breton onion sellers sell this variety strung with raffia; they keep well and a couple of strings will last a winter.

SORREL See HERBS

SPINACH **Spinach roulade p78, Spinach and cheese pies p77** Steam, add butter, salt and nutmeg – or purée with a little cream to accompany white fish.

SPRING GREEN Spring greens are the first cabbages of the year, their hearts tender with bright green loosely-formed leaves. Peel off any tough outer leaves, slice across and steam or boil. Serve with butter and seasoning. Excellent flavour.

SPRING ONION Onions that have not yet grown into their adult personas.

SQUASH **Baked squash with Parmesan p15** Gem is a summer squash. Over recent years a myriad of colourful varieties have appeared in the shops and in veg boxes, most of which are ready for autumn roasting or boiling. Basic methods include chopping, de-seeding, painting with olive or vegetable oil and roasting in a medium to hot oven until tender – about 45 minutes. The flesh can either be eaten from the skin, or removed and mashed with salt and pepper and butter. Most popular varieties include acorn and butternut squash.

STRAWBERRY **Eton Mess p79** June, Wimbledon – sweet fruit plucked warm from the plant, delivering a fragrance like no other fruit. Definitely not large, hard, tasteless fruits spirited into shops and markets at Christmas to whet our visual appetites but little else.

SWEDE A kindly, two-tone winter root vegetable with its purple and cream exterior. Peel, steam and mash with lots of butter, salt and pepper, or mix with carrot, a small potato and a fistful of chopped parsley and do precisely the same thing. Dice a small chunk into lamb stew with carrot.

SWEET POTATO Related only distantly to the potato. As the name suggests, it has a sweet flavour and is increasingly favoured in UK cuisine, served boiled of in small roasted chunks. Although sometimes called yam, there is not a close botanical connection.

TOMATO **Tomato, thyme and goat's cheese tart p82** Tomatoes are fruits rather than vegetables, but with lower sugar content and useful acidity they're well suited to savoury dishes. They were once known as the Love Apple and hailed originally from the Andes. It goes without saying these fruits are finest when bought seasonally. I like to brush past the plant near our back door and release the slightly metallic smell of their leaves, so redolent of summer.

TURNIP Use big turnips in small quantities. Young turnips that pulled from the ground around the end of June and in July are a delicious and delicate vegetable. Peel and cook whole, steam or boil. Eat hot with butter and chopped chives, or cold in salad.

UGLI FRUIT This is a Jamaican Tangelo, a hybridization of grapefruit, orange and tangerine.

VICTORIA PLUM, see PLUM

WATERCRESS **Watercress mousse p85, Watercress sauce p86** Semi-aquatic plant, strong peppery leaves and full of useful vitamins, particularly A and C. Excellent with game birds.

WATERMELON Eat for its beauty and refreshing qualities. Chill and cut chunks into salads. Thread on a kebab stick with other fruits.

YAM Yam is not a sweet potato. Used in many Caribbean dishes: peel and blanch for 20 minutes in salted water, then continue cooking as you would a potato.

ZUCCHINI see Courgette

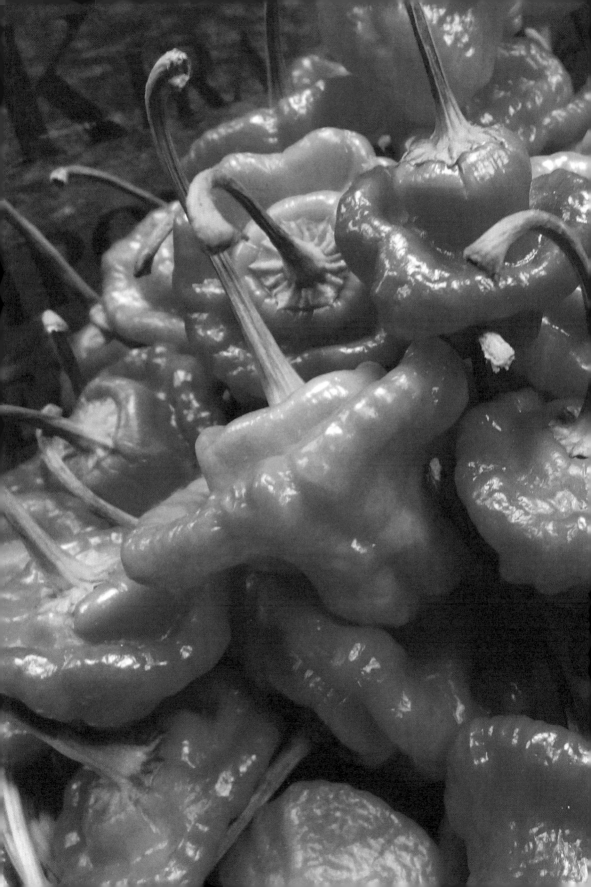

Herbs

Herbs are the brush stroke of the art master or the fine touch of the couturier; used in the right manner they possess significant powers of enhancement. Truthfully they should be another subject, another book, but here are some of the favourites available in the UK.

BASIL With its unmistakable fragrance, basil is essential in pesto and delicious with tomatoes. Plants thrive in a pot on the kitchen window sill and will regenerate as and when their leaves are nabbed for the cooking pot.

BAY Savoury, aromatic leaf; creating a casserole without one would be indefensible.. Will grow in a modest pot in the garden and make few demands on the gardener.

BORAGE Borage for beauty with its intense blue flower; use in Pimms, salads and on puddings. Bees love it too. Summer flowering.

CHILLI Read the labels! Impact varies from mild as in cayenne chilli to medium jalapeños to ferociously hot habaneros.

CHIVES Will grow in sun and shade. Snippets of fresh chives transform soups into super-soups and round off Hollandaise sauce with their delicacy.

CORIANDER The smell of coriander is emotive; sometimes appetizingly exotic, sometimes rancid. But a fistful of fresh chopped coriander on a curry or spiced dish works an effective catalyst, enhancing the impact of other spices, whilst simultaneously modifying its own pungency.

DILL The feathery fronds of aniseed-flavoured dill compliment fish dishes, equally such things as pickled herring and Danish-style cucumber.

FENNEL Fennel leaf grows from the fennel bulb and is similar to the feathery dill leaf, both visually and in flavour.

LAVENDER Lavender flowers infuse their fragrance into custards, cakes and ice cream. Steep a pint of warm milk with 3-4 flower heads for about an hour and strain before use – or put sugar for cake-making into a screw top jar with a few flowers.

MARJORAM A meaty herb, good for stews and soups; very similar to oregano.

MINT There is a mint for every day of the week; spearmint, apple mint, peppermint, Corsican mint, chocolate mint, variegated mint. Mint for mint sauce, mint for tea. Revitalizing draughts of menthol exude from this lovely herb.

NASTURTIUM Peppery edible leaves with radiantly decorative and edible flowers.

OREGANO Spicy, savoury; see the family resemblance with marjoram. Bees love the flowers.

PARSLEY FLAT LEAF Delicious fresh grassy flavour, adds colour, taste and is a good source of vitamin C.

PARSLEY CURLEY LEAF Take a good big bunch, chop and fry in hot vegetable oil until sea green and crisp; sprinkle on casseroles or sauces with fish. Has an excellent seaweed-like taste, akin to Japanese kombu.

RAMSONS *alias* wild garlic; the plants have prolific crowns of white flowers and broad leaves that flower in early spring and fill woodland air with their garlicky aroma. Chop the leaves into salads or make wild garlic soup.

ROCKET Peppery-tasting leaf similar in shape to a dandelion; perks up a salad and pretties up a plate.

ROSEMARY A bush with Mediterranean origins and a Mediterranean warmth; the needles infuse piquancy into lamb and chicken dishes – and add a herby robustness if finely chopped and scattered on crushed potatoes baked with a little olive oil and sea salt. Don't overdo quantities, it's punchy.

SAGE Sage-and-onion stuffing. Also used in herbal medicine.

SORREL Sorrel should be named The Disappearing Herb. A moderate bunch will vanish to an unprepossessing sludge when cooked, but it adds a superb lemon-sharpness to sauces for fish and chicken, and is equally effective in soup. It grows so easily, sprouting from knobbly, perennial roots, yet is hard to buy in UK.

TARRAGON Redolent of aniseed and liquorice; excellent in chicken and fish dishes, or add a few of the leaves to salad. Elegant in Hollandaise sauce.

THYME If you have a small outdoor area, please grow thyme, for bees and for the kitchen. A sprig of thyme is as essential to the stew pot as is a bay leaf; steam a chicken with lemon thyme, onion, carrot and bay and the flavours will astound.

Thanks

Nothing is ever a solo effort, and so it is with *A Veg for All Seasons*. Stephen Morris, designer and great friend, has woven his magic on a pile of recipes and photographs and turned them into a handsome compilation. Without his skill and humour there would be no book. The title is derived second hand from the late George Baker, actor and enthusiastic cook; George and his family were part of my life in my restaurant years; George wrote *A Cook for All Seasons*, a spin-off from the title of Robert Bolt's famous play. To be the husband of a food writer means you sometimes have to eat the same dish on several consecutive nights in order to 'get it right'; Nicholas has done this fairly uncomplainingly. My neighbour Kate Skillman has fulfilled the invaluable task of being chief taster over the garden wall. Clive and Wanda Owen and Jennifer and Michael Caola have produced perfect locations, allotments and gardens respectively. Reg the Veg, *alias* the Hagon family and their delightful assistants who were the catalysts for this book and a fount of information – and who be selling it in their shop:
Reg the Veg
6 Boyce's Avenue,
Clifton Village,
Bristol BS8 4AA
0117 970 6777

Thank you to all.

Andrea Leeman

E: andreavegforallseasons@btinternet.com

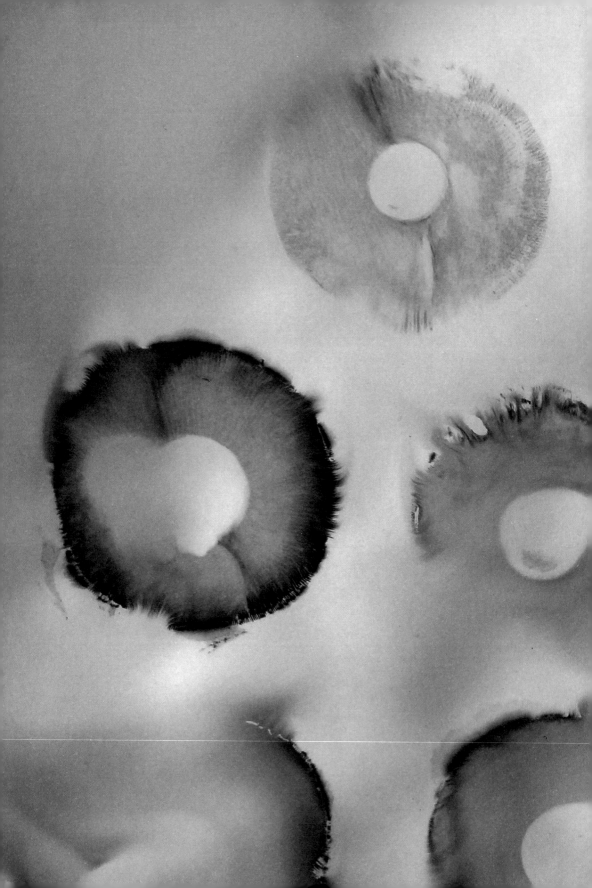